99

FEB 1 5

Senses in My World

Smelling

by Martha E. H. Rustad

Bullfrog Books

Ideas for Parents and Teachers

Bullfrog Books let children practice reading informational text at the earliest reading levels. Repetition, familiar words, and photo labels support early readers.

Before Reading

- Ask the child to think about senses. Ask: What do you smell at home or school?

- Look at the picture glossary together. Read and discuss the words.

Read the Book

- "Walk" through the book and look at the photos. Let the child ask questions. Point out the photo labels.

- Read the book to the child, or have him or her read independently.

After Reading

- Prompt the child to think more. Ask: What do you smell around you? How does smelling help you learn?

Bullfrog Books are published by Jump!
5357 Penn Avenue South
Minneapolis, MN 55419
www.jumplibrary.com

Library of Congress Cataloging-in-Publication Data

Rustad, Martha E. H. (Martha Elizabeth Hillman), 1975- author.
  Smelling / by Martha E.H. Rustad.
    pages cm. — (Senses in my world)
  Summary: "This photo-illustrated book for young readers describes how smelling works and what we learn about our surroundings through our sense of smell" — Provided by publisher.
  Audience: Ages 5-8.
  Audience: K to grade 3.
  Includes bibliographical references and index.
  ISBN 978-1-62031-117-2 (hardcover) —
  ISBN 978-1-62496-184-7 (ebook) —
  ISBN 978-1-62031-151-6 (paperback)
  1. Smell — Juvenile literature.
  2. Nose — Juvenile literature. I. Title.
  QP458.R87 2015
  612.8'6—dc23

                                        2013049896

Series Editor: Rebecca Glaser
Series Designer: Ellen Huber
Book Designer: Anna Peterson
Photo Researcher: Kurtis Kinneman

Photo Credits: Dreamstime/Tatyana Gladskikh, 11; Dreamstime/Tofuxs, 10; Getty Images/Fuse, 12 (inset), 12–13, 23br; iStock/Imgorthand, 14–15; iStock/Lepro, 17; Shutterstock/3445128471, 14 (inset), 23tr; Shutterstock/Alila Medical Media, 22; Shutterstock/CLIPAREA l Custom Media, 7 (inset), 23tl; Shutterstock/gosphotodesign, 6–7, 23bl; Shutterstock/Marco Mayer, 1; Shutterstock/Marques, 20 (inset); Shutterstock/Niki Crucillo, 19 (inset); Shutterstock/Nito, 16; Shutterstock/Paleka, 3; Shutterstock/Samuel Borges Photography, 4, 5; Shutterstock/Smit, 8 (inset); Shutterstock/Timmary, 24; Shutterstock/Valeriy Lebedev, cover; Shutterstock/wavebreakmedia, 20–21; SuperStock/AsiaPix, 8–9; SuperStock/Blend Images, 18–19

Printed in the United States of America at Corporate Graphics, in North Mankato, Minnesota.
6-2014
10 9 8 7 6 5 4 3 2 1

Table of Contents

How Do We Smell?

We use our noses to smell.

How does our sense
of smell work?

scent
bits

Tiny bits of scent float
in the air.

The nose breathes in air.

The brain understands
the bits as smells.

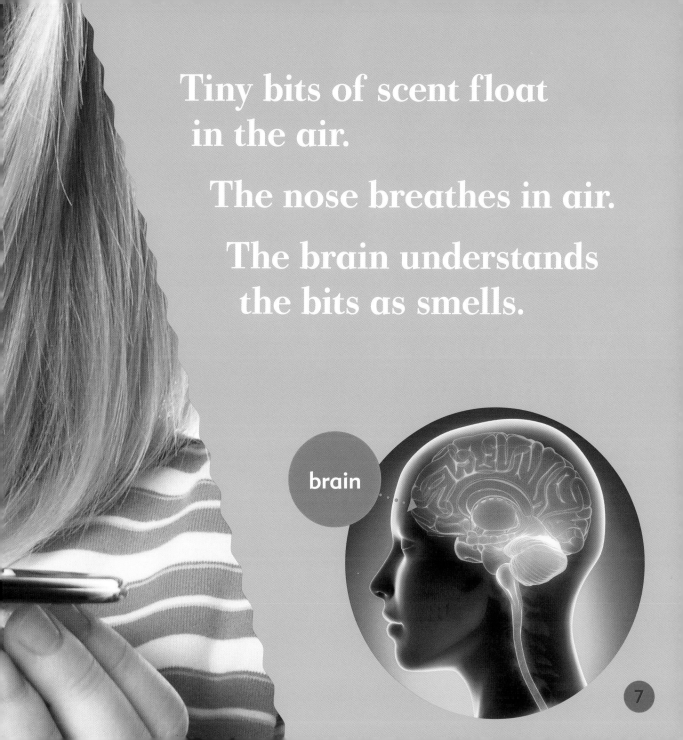

brain

What things do
we smell?

Sean smells pizza.

Yum!

He knows what
is for supper.

He knows the
fire is started.

Iva smells flowers.

Sniff!

She knows spring
is here.

Eli smells his stinky feet.

Ew!

He knows he needs
a bath.

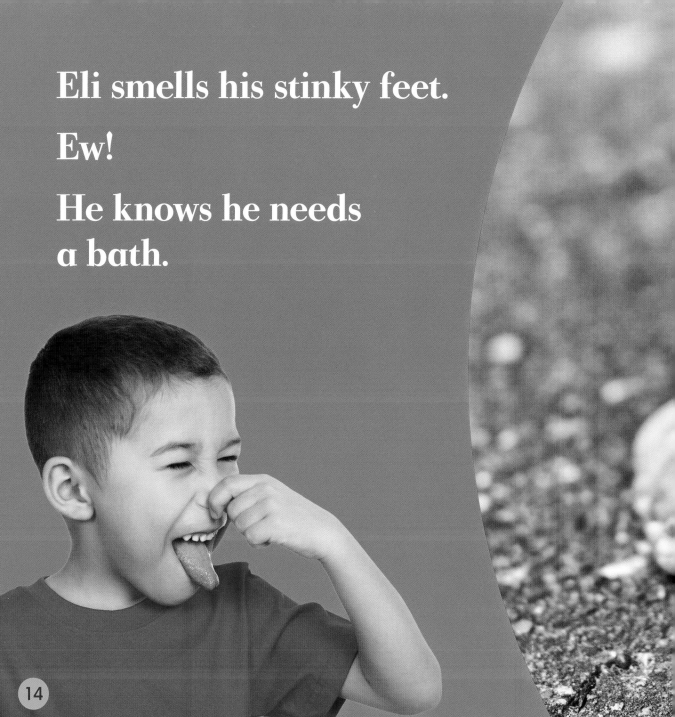

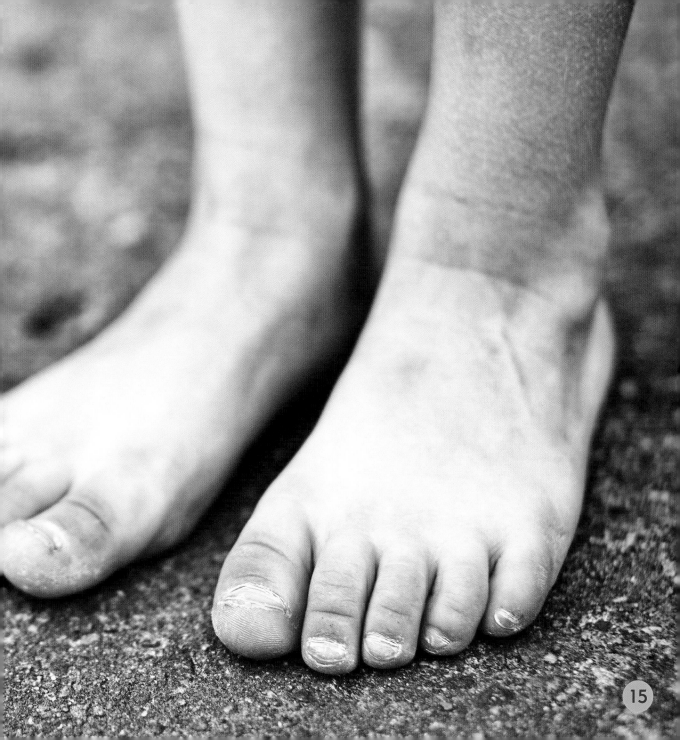

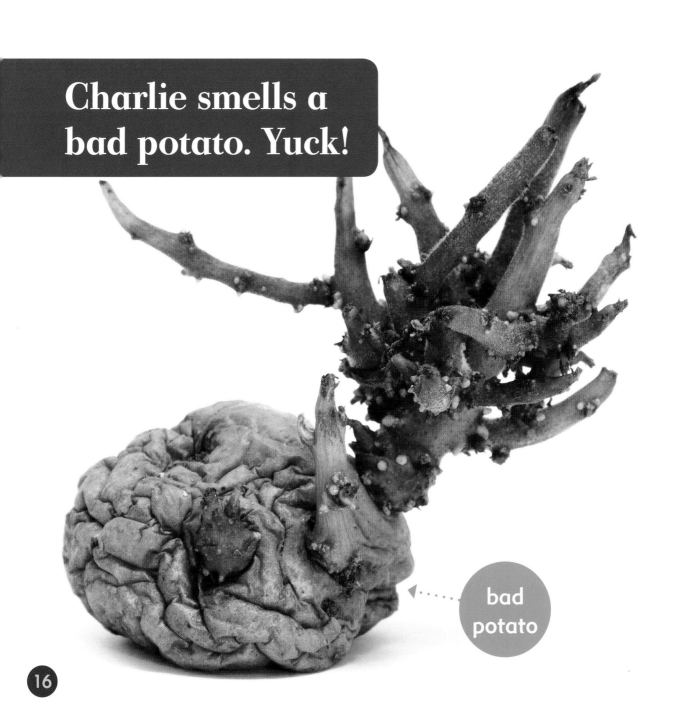

Charlie smells a bad potato. Yuck!

bad potato

He knows not to eat it.

Anna cannot smell.

She has a cold.

Her nose is stuffed up.

Achoo!

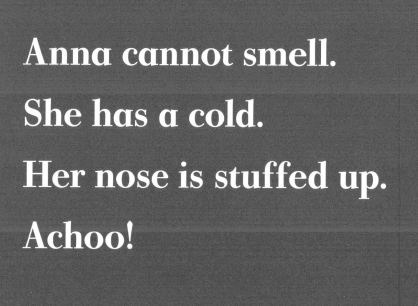

What things do you smell?
What do they tell you?

Parts of the Nose

olfactory bulb
A part of the brain that understands smells.

nasal cavity
An empty space inside your nose.

nostril
One of the two holes in your nose; scent bits and air go in your nostrils.

Picture Glossary

brain
A body part in your head that helps you think and understand.

scent
A smell.

breathe
To bring air into and out of your body.

sense
A way of knowing about things around you; you have five senses.

Index

To Learn More

Learning more is as easy as 1, 2, 3.

1) Go to www.factsurfer.com

2) Enter "smelling" into the search box.

3) Click the "Surf" button to see a list of websites.

With factsurfer.com, finding more information is just a click away.